How to Stretch for Ma
Your Ultimate Flexibility

"Unlock the Potential in Your Body...!"

Phil Pierce

For a Free Martial Arts guide visit:
http://www.BlackBeltFit.com

What Can You Get From This Book?

- **Do you know the shocking research changing everything we know about stretching?!**

- **The most common Killer mistake and which stretches are actually reducing your power?!**

- **Do you know the fool-proof exercise that is more effective than 90% of so-called 'warm-ups'?**

- **How to Push your limits and stay safe?**

- **Why you may be so inflexible at the moment?**

- **Is Heat or Cold more effective to treat injury?**

- **What specific stretches work your whole body?**

- **Do you know the 'trick' to true flexibility?**

The simple aim of this book is to unlock your body's potential and show you the powerful and effective stretches and warm up exercises that take your flexibility to the next level! (And reveal the surprising mistakes you may already be making!)

The techniques and methods within this guide are all designed to be easy to follow, simple to perform and allow you to really maximise your Martial Arts, Fitness or training regime through improved suppleness and reduced risk of injury.

Whether you are just starting out as a beginner or someone with years of experience, discover how to get a powerful boost in your performance today…

Contents

Free Bonus Book!

Grab your Completely Free bonus book;
'How to Develop Power with Plyometrics' now!

Just head over to my site:

www.BlackBeltFit.com

Claim your copy now!

From the Author

If you could go back and give yourself one piece of advice what would it be?

Over 15 years of training around the world I have been lucky enough to sample a huge variety of different Martial Arts, Fitness Systems and Self Defense practices.

I never claim to have mastered every one of them – after all, the journey is often more important than the destination – but I have enjoyed every moment and I've learned a lot along the way. There is one lesson that sticks out more than others however.

If there's one thing I wish I could tell the younger me it would be;

"Don't skip the warm-up"

I'll spare you the unpleasant details of my previous injuries but suffice to say they have been many and painful!

It's easy when we are full of energy and enthusiasm (and youth!) to jump straight into an activity at full pelt, but it's exactly this kind of approach that ultimately puts us out of commission long term. Not only this, but leaping into action without sufficient warm up is putting a serious dampener on your performance from the outset.

Warming up and Stretching is ESSENTIAL.

Not; "nice to have", not; "if I have time".

Essential.

If you are serious about improving your performance, reducing injury risk and really gaining an advantage in your training, then allowing a 5-10 minute period of gradual Warm-Up before each session should be top of your list.

My approach to warm-up is now pretty much compulsory. It doesn't have to be much, but I've found that allowing a short introductory time before any exercise session has made a world of difference.

Even if you've never trained a day of Martial Arts in your life, and don't intend to, the simple act of loosening the muscles of your body, as part of a regular routine, can really help you achieve a happier, healthy and more relaxed life!

The simple tips in this guide cover a broad range of full body stretches and advice for Martial Arts, Fitness and General Well-Being; all designed to unlock the potential in your body and allow you to improve your performance, starting right now...

- Phil Pierce

What is Real Flexibility?

"Moving your body through its best potential range of movement…"

Unfortunately most people give little thought to flexibility training. From outside appearances stretching won't help you lose weight, get stronger, or give you the chiseled abs you've seen on TV.

Which of course raises the question…why should I bother?

The first thing to understand is that flexibility is actually just as important as things like strength and endurance, especially so in the case of the Martial Artist or fitness fan.

Bottom line; if you aren't flexible, you've already put a huge limit your athletic ability not to mention the increase to your risk of serious injury. Flexibility is extra valuable when taking part in any activity that places additional stress on the joints and muscles like kicking and punching.

Incorporating a stretching program into your training regime will not only increase agility but also improve balance and overall wellness. As a bonus it also helps to flush the toxins that can build up in muscles during physical exertion.

If none of that appeals to you then consider that a more flexible muscle at rest will contract faster and with greater force when in use, allowing you to use the **maximum amount of power** – often calculated as Speed x Strength.

A flexibility improvement program will increase your range of motion and help it stay there, reduce stiffness and soreness, plus massively reduce the risk of injury during training. A perfect combination for anyone!

Why am I so Inflexible at the moment?

Are you stiffer than a board and wondering why?

Over the years there have been a hundred and one reasons given for an individual's flexibility – or lack of. Usually a mixture of the truth and some far-fetched excuse.

"The Wheat in my diet means I can't lift my leg that high these days..."

- a genuine comment from a fellow student, some years ago.

Simply put, research has shown that flexibility is determined by a combination of the following;

- **Physical build, (and genes)**
  (If both of your parents were Olympic gymnasts you have a good chance at inheriting some of this natural muscular ability)

- **Age**
  (Perhaps not surprisingly Age is a big factor)
- **Overall health of your body and specifically ligaments, tendons, and muscles.**
  (If you smoke 50 a-day and have a poor diet expect this to be reflected in your flexibility)

As we get older and, ultimately less active, our flexibility reduces naturally, hence muscles become tight through disuse. (Think of a car engine. Unused for weeks on end it seizes up and becomes harder to start)

Unfortunately we live in an age where huge percentages of people work in office or computer based environments. This lifestyle, often combined with little exercise in our free time, leads to long term deterioration of our health and flexibility. This sedentary (Couch Potato) lifestyle will cause your muscles to tighten and atrophy – waste away. Stretching is one of the most important things you can do for your long-term health.

A small but regular exercise system that includes flexibility training can help to reduce or at least slow down the process and improve well-being massively.

Numerous fitness, Martial Arts guides and training systems are available (You can check out a couple of my own on Amazon) but even if you don't follow a fixed system the benefits of stretching can be seen by all, at home, in the office or in the Dojo.

No matter how "tight" you feel now, it's easy to drastically improve your flexibility and overall health starting now!

How Does Stretching Enhance Flexibility?

Have you ever wondered why people tend to experience reduced flexibility as they become older or less active? The culprit is something known as Myotatic Reflex. It is also commonly referred to as the stretch reflex. The purpose of the reflex is to safeguard your body against strains or tears that might otherwise result from overextended muscles.

It works both for, and against us, in most cases of physical exertion.

The reflex is in effect in every muscle within your body. When you make an abrupt or exaggerated movement the Myotatic Reflex acts as a resistance, limiting the movement within the muscle. You have likely observed this in the tension felt through a stretch, or high kick. Like any reflex it can be both a blessing and a curse. Some athletes in fact find it a hindrance in the way it can sometimes limit their training abilities.

However, it also ensures that progress is found gradually and therefore more safely.

You can use this reflex as an advantage when training your body for martial arts. It is possible to work beyond the Myotatic Reflex, but it takes patient conditioning to teach your body that it is ok to stretch beyond the usual limits. That's not to say the stretches need to all be slow and gradual, just that progress in overcoming this reflex should not be rushed. It will happen but patience is most definitely a virtue here.

In order to effectively train in this manner your movements must be patient, gentle, and methodical.

Forcing any muscle beyond the point of comfort will only result in injury and may even create scar tissue, or weaken the muscle, which will ultimately limit your flexibility and increase the time needed for recovery. Plan on enhancing your flexibility over a number of months rather than days. Slow and steady should be your mantra for success.

Forms of Stretching

There are four main different types of stretches you will encounter. Each holds its own benefits and limitations making them all necessary for your martial arts or fitness training. Mixing up a variety of stretches allows for a well-balanced routine putting the whole body through its paces.

Below you will find an overview of each variety.

Static:

These kinds of stretches are somewhat of an old –school approach to flexibility, they are slow and require control. Static Stretches work by gradually extending a group of muscles just to the point of discomfort. Each stretch is held for a certain count. For the best results, try to keep the muscle relaxed. Gradual movements can be made towards a deepened stretch, but not to the point of pain.

NOTE: Latest research shows Static stretching has fewer benefits than originally thought. See the article "The Surprising Discovery…" later in this guide.

Ballistic:

Best known for being a bouncing stretch, the ballistic variety is often presented as the opposite of static. Here movement is used to increase the participant's flexibility. Example: Swinging ones arms outward is considered a ballistic stretch because it relies on momentum.

Dynamic:

If static is the opposite of ballistic then dynamic is her sister. Each dynamic stretch performed is customized to the demands of the activity at hand, in this case martial arts. It is wise to begin each stretch at a slowed pace, to ensure proper posture before increasing the velocity of the movement. The goal is a smooth rhythmic motion that does not overwhelm the muscle. *Caution: Dynamic stretching requires guidance and supervision by a professional. Incorrect stances or pushing too far can result in serious injury. Also avoid going into any sort of bouncing movement.*

Dynamic Stretching has recently been proven to be the most effective form of warm up in most exercise scenarios. The use of body motion to increase blood flow and reduce stiffness has, in many modern studies, proven to show far greater results than traditional methods of static stretching.

Proprioceptive Neuromuscular Facilitation:

Also known as PNF or sometimes Muscle Energy work. Proprioceptive Neuromuscular Facilitation utilizes both the contraction and relaxation of a muscle to increase flexibility. These kinds of stretches stimulate a response by the nervous system that stops the muscle from contracting during a stretch.

Example: With help from a partner, lift one leg up just to that point of resistance. Then, press downward against your helper. First tighten and then relax the leg muscles. Finally stretch upward again and you will likely be able to go a bit beyond the original point of resistance.

The Power of Stretching with a Partner

If possible, working with a partner can be an important aid in improving flexibility through stretching exercises. Not only does their presence give you a body to offer resistance but most people find they work harder and push themselves more when they have someone else to encourage them.

It is a similar principle to fitness training or attending the gym. The presence of someone else – a friend or fellow Martial Arts student - pushes you to work harder, often subconsciously creating a mild sense of competition. Use this to your advantage and arrange a session of stretching before or after a Martial Arts class or training session.

You will find you are more consistent in sticking to your regime if it is shared with someone else because by nature we don't want to let someone we know down.

Here are a couple of examples of popular Martial Arts stretches greatly improved by including a partner. Many of the other exercises included in this guide can be adapted for two people. Consider how you might include someone else in your programme.

Outer Leg Swings

Start by facing your partner standing normally. One of you then takes half a step to the left before you both place your inner (closest) hand on each other's shoulder for support. Keeping the inner leg bent you both then take the outer leg back as straight as possible.
This outer leg is then swung straight up and back down ten times. The aim being to keep the leg as straight as possible while swinging. On the Eighth, Ninth and Tenth swing try to get the leg as high as comfortably possible for the most benefit.

Depending on ease of balance both partners can work the outer leg simultaneously or wait until the other has completed.

To swap legs one partner now takes a step to the right (the opposite direction) and the sequence is repeated on the other legs, still on the outside.

Variations:
By using a hand on the partners shoulder for stabilization a variety of leg swings can be completed to stretch different muscle groups.

- Swinging the leg sideways to 90 degrees and back down
- Swinging just the knee up to a chambered side kick position
- Swinging the leg straight back behind your body while looking over your shoulder

Partner V Stretch

Similar to the V stretch listed here this variation simply involves facing a partner while seated with your legs wide in the "V" shape making a diamond shape in the gap between you.
Pulling in close you can push your feet together and offer resistance but the best stretch is by carefully linking hands and rocking gently back and forth.

Note that slow gradual movements are key here to avoid injury. To enhance the stretch one partner can slowly pull the other down lower for a longer period; say 10 seconds, before switching it around

Variations

In a slightly tougher variation both partners keep their legs straight out ahead with soles of the feet touching. Both then reach to link hands and again slowly rock forward and back.
This exercises a different group of muscles to the V stretch but is extremely effective if completed correctly.

Knee Raises

As a great Warm up, or Cardio exercise on its own, Knee Raises mobilize the whole lower body in a high energy motion.

Stand facing your partner with feet approximately a shoulders width apart. Your partner then holds their hands out flat, palms facing the floor with elbows bent. (Palms should be roughly at waist height).

Set a 10, 20 or 30 second interval and jog on the spot raising your legs high on each stroke so that your knee just touches your partner's palm. The aim is either to complete as many touches in the given time as possible (a fairly intense Cardio exercise) or to complete a fixed amount at an average pace. (A gentler warm-up)

After the given time, swap sides and allow your partner to complete the knee raises while you hold your palms out.

Variations

The same exercise can be applied more specifically to Martial Arts by bringing the knees up and to the side of the body each time in a chambered side kick position for the chosen count or time.

The Shocking Discovery Changing Everything we know about Stretching! (A must read)

We live in an incredible time of sports sciences. An age where technology and the latest research has enabled us to measure the tiniest details of an individual's performance and track every slight movement during any event.

Whereas in the old days, recommendations for effectiveness were often based on anecdotes and hearsay from surly old 'experts', today we have the hard facts and figures backing up the claims, and revealing some surprising truths.

Experts in the field of kinesiology are now publishing strongly documented reports that indicate much of what we take for granted when training is actually outright wrong!

Although not related directly to flexibility, one fascinating revelation has been regarding the use of sneakers while running.

For example it was recently revealed through large scale studies of athletes at several Universities, including Harvard, that running barefoot has significant benefits over using footwear of any kind. That's right; those $100+ sneakers with air bubbles, ridges and suspension are statistically more likely to cause an injury to you than running around with your feet in the nude.

When running barefoot your foot strikes the ground in a more natural way. The toes splay correctly and the forefoot, instead of the heel, strikes the ground earlier generating a better form and typically reducing the risk of injury.

Not surprising when you consider that pre-historic man did just fine running around chasing Wooly Mammoths without expensive Nikes.

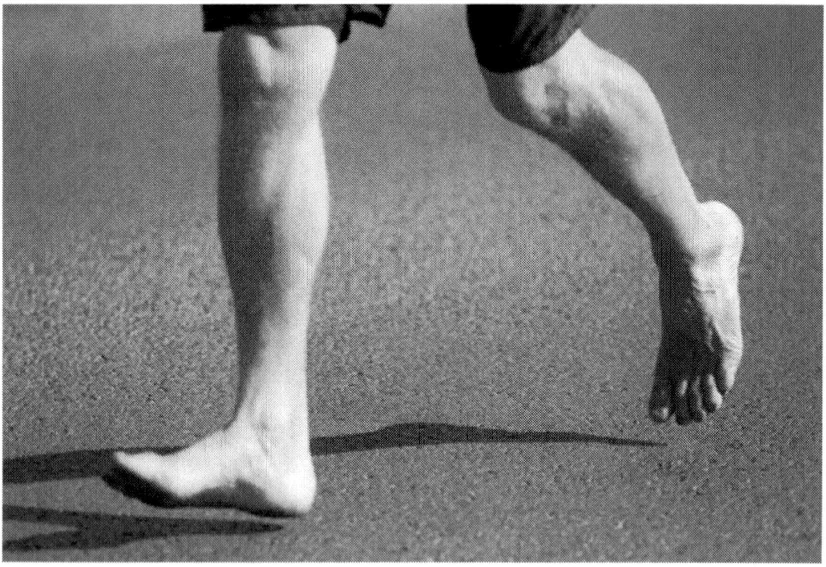

Now those of you coming from a traditional Martial Arts background, like Karate or Taekwondo, are probably feeling pretty smug right about now.

"We've always trained barefoot!" - I hear you say.

Well, while you may have made the correct choice in footwear, or lack of, there is an excellent chance you have been warming up and stretching incorrectly for years.

Yes, those Sports Science boffins have struck again, and this time it is the art of stretching that comes under scrutiny.

You see most of us have been doing the same type of limbering up since school. We'd stand in a freezing field pulling our legs left and right while a sadistic gym instructor prepared to force us on a freezing 6 mile run. (Well, that was my school experience anyway).

It turns out however that static stretches, the type where you stand and slowly pull a limb until you meet resistance, is not only useless in warming up the muscles but actually reduces the strength of that muscle's output for a short time afterwards!

A recent study carried out by the University of Nevada revealed that athletes produced less force from leg muscles after doing a series of static (traditional) stretches, than if they had done no stretching at all!

Other research has shown up to a 30 percent decrease in muscle strength after static stretching and that static stretches can even affect other limbs. (In theory due to the impact on the central nervous system as a whole).

Shocking Stuff!

A "neuromuscular inhibitory response" is the culprit; effectively your body and muscles reacting negatively and resisting the static stretch.

While you might feel more flexible initially, the actual muscular output is lessened and you've simply increased mental tolerance to the sensation.

Instead all studies now point to Dynamic Stretching and Dynamic Warm Ups as the optimal way to prepare for activity.

Dynamic Stretching/Warm Up:

- Increases Blood Flow
- Works full range of motion
- Increases Power
- Improves Flexibility

In fact Dynamic Stretches and warm ups were shown in a recent CDC study to cut injury rates by around 50% compared with the alternatives.

Exercises

Bear Crawl

There are a number of Static, Dynamic and Ballistic Stretches included in this guide but any full body exercise can work well. An increasingly popular example is the "Spider-man" or as it's known in some Martial Arts circles the "Bear-Crawl".

Simply drop to all fours and walk the length of the gym or training hall then back again. This engages most of the body and is an excellent all-body dynamic warm up.

Reaching Leg Swings

Another, slightly different, approach to the leg swings listed in this guide; simply walk a length of the gym while swinging one leg at a time straight out in front, toes pointed skyward. With the opposite hand swing the arm and reach for the raised toes as you step.

Complete a few times or for a length of the gym or training hall.

Not Quite Down and Out

It's worthwhile remembering that static stretches aren't completely without value. Sure they aren't going to help you immediately before an event (in fact they can make things worse!) but they do have a place <u>after</u> exercise to help muscles remain loose, retain length and ensure blood flow.

How to Warm-Up Properly: A foolproof tactic

Do what you do.

While specific stretches aid in preparing localized muscle groups for action, and reduce stiffness and tension after an event, warming up as a whole is just as important to introduce the body to the activity it is about to undertake.

The latest research and scientific developments may be changing our opinions about traditional stretches and how effective (or wasteful) static stretches really are but interestingly these studies have also revealed the most effective way to warm- up in general for an activity and lucky for us it's very simple;

"Do what you do"

That is, most studies have now shown that the best way to warm up for a specific activity is to do that activity - though at a reduced intensity.

It's not rocket science, and yet for years all sorts of new and trendy pseudo-science approaches to warming up have been adopted in different fitness circles.

Thankfully common sense is finally getting the backup it deserves from concrete results and we are now seeing some sensible approaches to warm up exercises that are non-technical and actually good for your body!

Simply put;

If you are a runner, to warm up you need to run.

If you are a swimmer, then swim.

A Martial Artist should make a few kicks and punches. (Depending on your style)

Intensity is Key

There is a slight caveat to this approach though, in that you don't throw yourself into the activity at full strength straight away. That kind of shock to the system does no good for your body. Instead introduce the exercise at a lower intensity, then a slightly higher intensity, then the full speed, normal activity.

For example, a warm up for runners might be;

- 5 minutes walking at a quick pace - 30% of normal running speed
- 5 minutes jogging slightly faster – 50% of normal running speed
- Finally begin to pick up the pace and run at normal speed.

A simple warm up for Martial Artists;

- Light Shadow Boxing/Sparring for 2 mins
- Slightly faster sparring for 2 mins
- Full Normal Speed sparring (with a partner if needed)

The times have been slightly reduced for sparring because it is already a quite intense exercise

This simple approach of "Do what you do" makes it easy to warm up safely and since you already know the activity there are no complicated techniques for you to work out or potentially get wrong.

Your activity at 20-30% intensity (for 5-10 mins)

To
Your activity at 40-50% intensity (for 5-10 mins)
To
Your activity at normal full intensity

Give it a go!

Hot or Cold for Muscle Recovery? (and How To Cool Down)

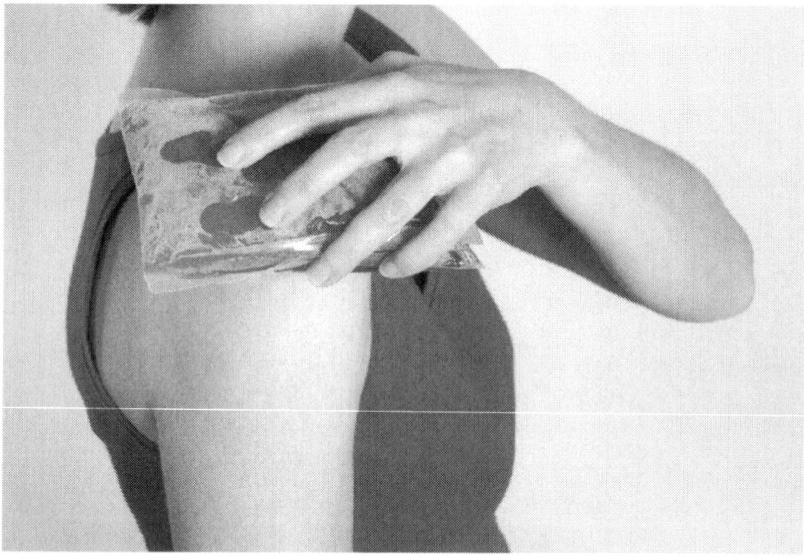

One of the longest standing debates amongst Martial Artists, and fitness enthusiasts in general, has been the use of heat or Ice post-event to aid in muscle recovery and injury treatment. Both have their benefits and both are frequently touted as the savior of the exhausted athlete in treating 'DOMS', aka Delayed Onset Muscle Soreness.

So which one works?

Warm/Cool Down

Firstly remember that warming down after exercise is just as important as warming up and yet this part is frequently overlooked. Instead of collapsing in heap on the floor or just jumping in the car to go home, try to keep the muscles active for a short period (approx 5-10 minutes) after they have been engaged in intense exercise.

Gradually reducing intensity allows toxins to flush from the tissues and prevents the cramps sometimes associated with a sudden stop in activity. It also allows the heart and circulatory system to transition back to rest, avoiding dizziness or potential nausea.

From a flexibility viewpoint a gradual reduction also prevents the muscles getting tight too quickly and encourages longer term elasticity.

An incredibly simple approach to cooling down is to simply walk around the gym, training hall, parking lot or wherever, for around 5 to 10 minutes after exercise. This low intensity movement keeps the blood flowing, helps prevent blood 'pooling' and prevents the buildup of waste products like Lactic Acid.

First Ice, then Heat

Most studies have shown that while both heat and Ice are effective in treating muscles, they work in very different ways and as such should be used at different times.

Ice has the cooling effect of constricting blood vessels and reducing inflammation. Since Muscle soreness is typically triggered by micro-damage to the muscle fibers, applying Ice soon after an event reduces swelling and improves recovery time.

Studies have shown that athletes taking an ice bath post-exercise typically showed a 20 percent reduction in Muscle soreness the next day.

If an ice bath is unrealistic (and let's face it, for most of us it is!) then a similar localized effect can be achieved through using an ice pack, or if you are really on a budget, some frozen vegetables on an inflamed area.

IMPORTANT: If you do choose to use ice, never apply it directly to the skin. Wrap the ice pack, Frozen Peas or whatever you use, in a towel or cloth first. The aim is to cool the tissue down, not freeze it, which causes long term skin damage!

Heat on the other hand does the opposite. Applying a heat-pack to body tissues causes the blood vessels to dilate and increased circulation to the area.

Heat is best applied much later, after the initial swelling or inflammation has gone down. (Typically 48 hours + after event).

If the muscles are still sore, but not displaying any obvious signs of damage, a heat pack applied twice-a-day for 15-20mins at a time can help increase the circulation, which in turn relaxes the area and brings increased nutrients through the blood supply. This again can speed up recovery time and reduce long-term damage.

IMPORTANT: As with Ice, high temperature heat packs should never be directly applied to the skin. Wrap these in a towel or cloth to prevent burning.

How to Stay Safe While Stretching

Although stretching is a great part of any conditioning program, it needs to be done right in order to avoid getting hurt. Follow this list of guidelines to ensure that your practice remains both effective and injury-free.

- As with any new fitness routine, talk with your doctor before beginning. It may be important to ensure that there are no reasons why such a program would be dangerous or detrimental to your health.

- Before stretching, warm your muscles through at least five minutes of a gentle activity such as walking, or jogging.

- Use a few minutes of stretches to prepare your body for other physical activities. For the best results perform them between three and five times each week.

- Never use abrupt, sudden, or jolting movements. Instead make sure your stretches are smooth and mindful of the resistance point for each muscle group.

- Remember to breathe. Remain relaxed, calm, inhale and exhale with each stretch. Try not to hold your breath.

- After holding a stretch to your point of resistance, try to stretch a bit further for up to half a minute.

- There is no need to rush. It may take some time to notice a significant difference, but you will eventually. Stay patient and trust the process.

- Throughout each stretch imagine the muscle group being worked as it lengthens and gains an increased range of motion.

- Never force a stretch beyond your resistance point which will be signalled by that delicate sense of pulling against the movement in question. Do not push past the point of discomfort.

- If you notice any painful sensations stop the stretch immediately and consult your doctor. Not heeding this advice could lead to long term muscle damage.

Effective Exercises

The exercises presented here are split between the upper and lower body areas. These are followed by a variety of compound stretches which will work a combination of regions. For our purposes the upper body region is defined as the neck, arms, shoulders and torso. The lower body region refers to the hips, thighs, calves, ankles and feet. You will find a variety of stretches for each target group. Choose the stretches that you are most comfortable with, but be sure to change up your routine every few weeks for the best results.

Remember to be patient as it may take months before you reach your goals, but you will get there through dedicated practice. Go slow until you are sure you have found the proper form to avoid injury. As mentioned in the safety guidelines, you should stop and consult a doctor at the first hint of pain.

How to Stretch the Upper Body

Neck:

Looking Left & Right

Begin upright, or relaxed in a chair. Gently move your head toward the right, as far as it will comfortably go. Stay like this for about 15 seconds before moving your head all the way to the left. Hold here for another 15 seconds before returning to start to complete one rep.

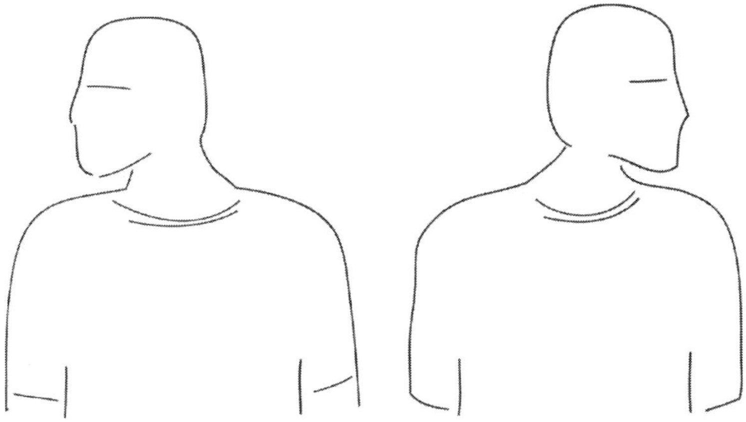

Neck Flex and Extension

Start out standing or sitting in a natural posture. Gradually drop your chin down in the direction of your chest. Hold this stretch for about 15 seconds. Then, come back to start and extend you neck backward to that point of resistance. Stay in this position for 15 seconds before coming back up to starting position.

Arms & Shoulders:

The arm and shoulder region is an area that accumulates a lot of tension in everyday life let alone through Martial Arts or fitness training. The stretches here are perfect for improving muscle condition and those training in styles that heavily emphasize punching and arm techniques, like Wing Chun and Boxing.

Back, Up, and Over

Stand with your feet spread to about shoulder width and arms down at your sides. Begin by swinging both arms up over your head, reach upward and lift onto the balls of your feet. Stretch your whole body from toe to fingertip. Bring your arms back using the same swinging motion but this time move backward and bend over as you come down to a flat footing. Once more, swing your arms up over the top and back down, as your bring your body into standing.

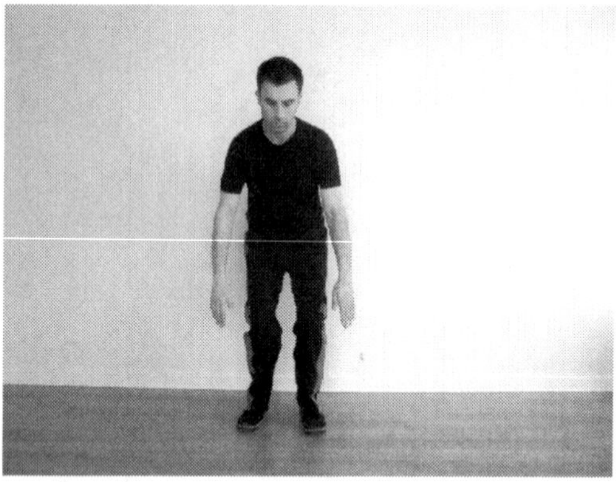

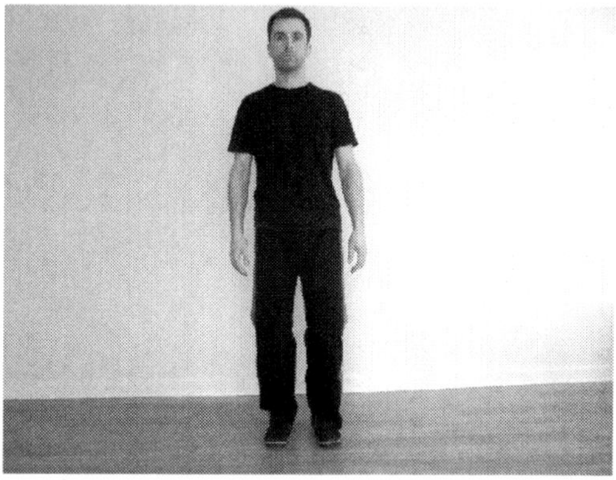

Swimming Stretch

Commence this stretch in an upright position, with feet spread to about shoulder width. Put your hands behind your back and intertwined as though you were holding your own hands. Extend the arms out so that they are fairly straight, but not so far that the elbows lock. Keeping the arms like this, lift them up and backward as far as you can comfortably reach. Now bend from your waist, moving both arms even further back. Hold this pose for about 15 seconds before relaxing back into your initial stance.

Chicken Wings

This one can be done either standing or in a seated position. In either case, bring your right hand toward your left shoulder, grabbing onto the elbow to ease it into place. Now place the right elbow behind your head and hold the stretch for about 15 seconds before repeating on the opposite side.

If you are able, try clasping your hands in the middle. If not, just perform the stretch to a comfortable point and hold for a few sconds.

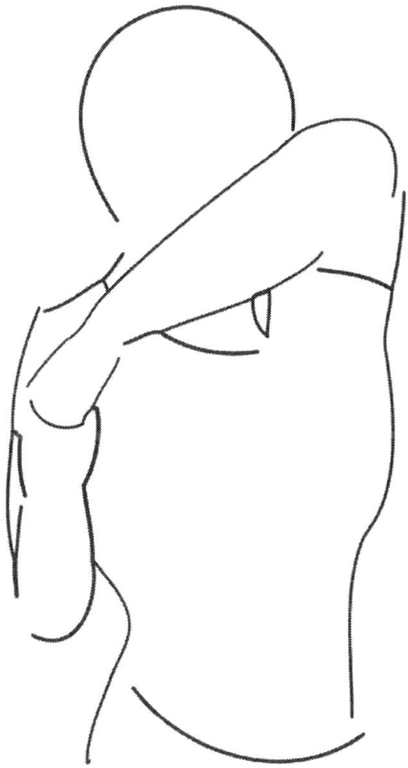

Basic Triceps Stretch

Position the palm of your right hand so that it rests against your back just a bit lower than your neck. The elbow should be aimed upward. Hold the elbow of your right arm in the palm of your left hand. Gradually press until you reach the point of resistance. Stay in this stretch for a count of 15 before switching to the other side and repeating.

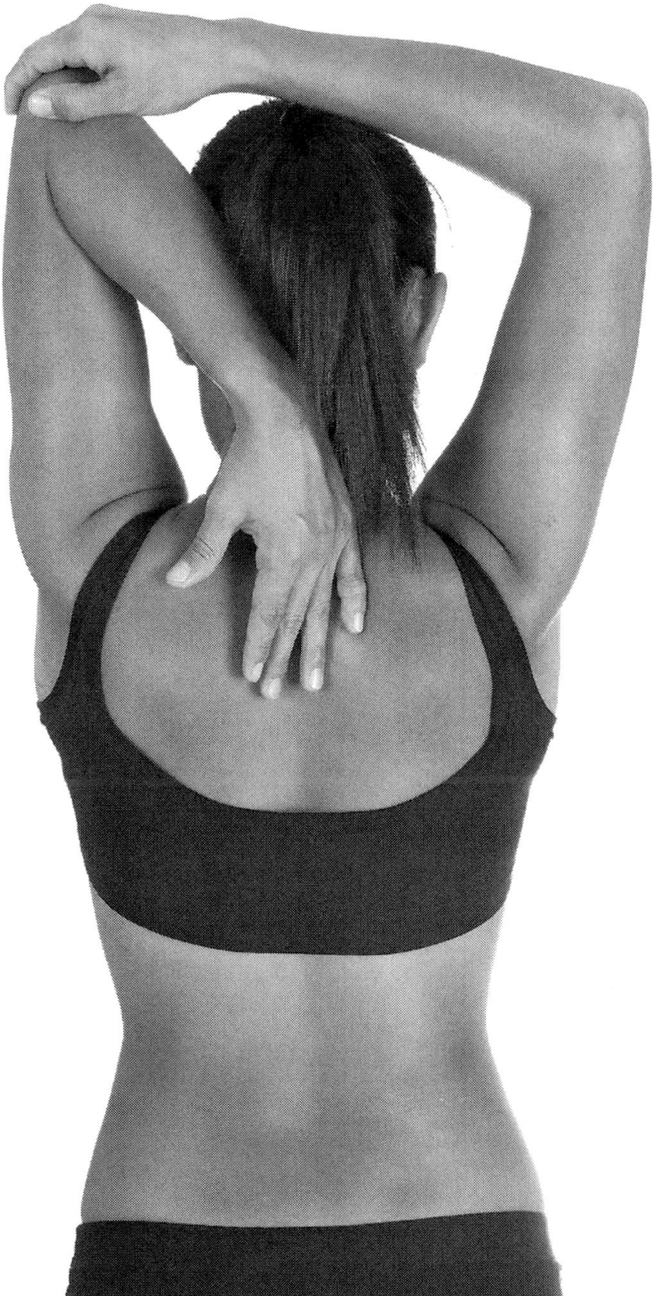

Bending Backward (Back-Bend)

To find your position for this stretch sit on the floor. Now straighten your legs and place the palms of your hands down behind you so that the fingers are pointed outward. Gently tip backward, allowing your hands to follow until you reach the point of resistance. Hold this pose for about 15 seconds before returning back to start.

Go slowly with this motion as the back can be a sensitive area.

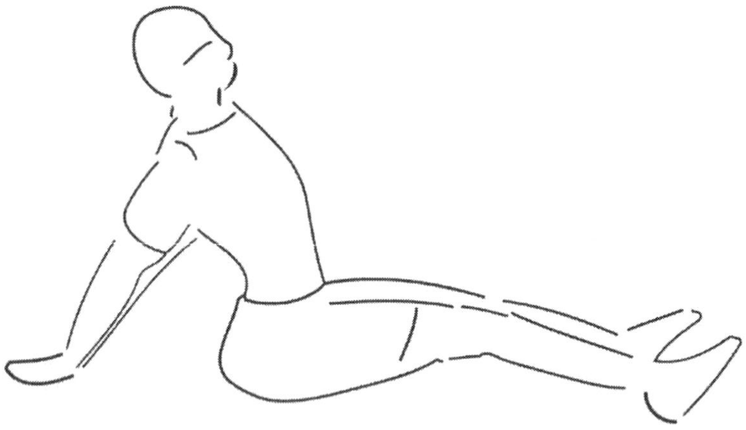

Two-handed Forearm Stretch

Straighten your right arm up in front of your body to about shoulder height. The palm should be open toward the floor. Bring up the left hand to grab the fingers of your right hand. Gradually ease the fingers backward so that you feel a slight stretch in your wrist and forearm. Count to 15 before relaxing back to your natural stance.

Remember to complete an equal number of repetitions on each side.

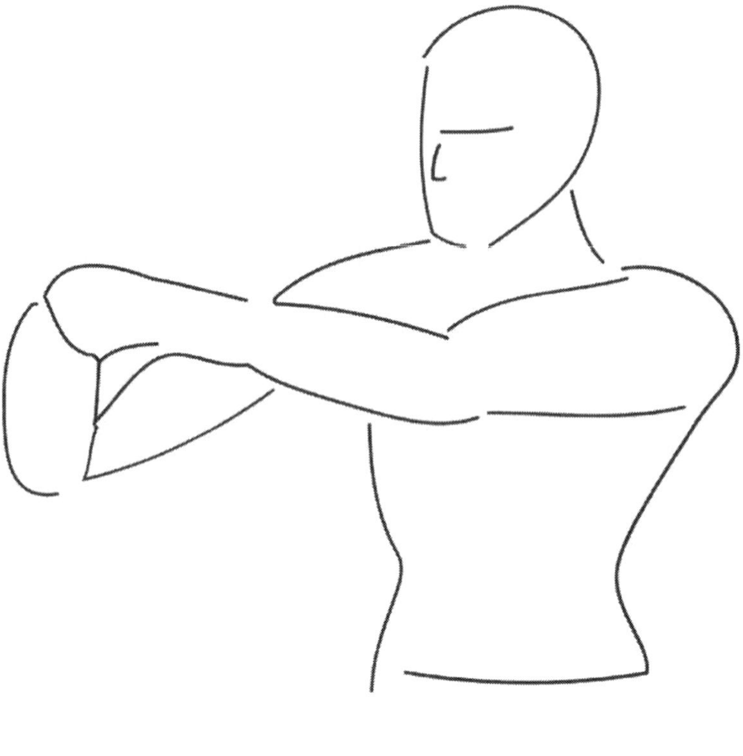

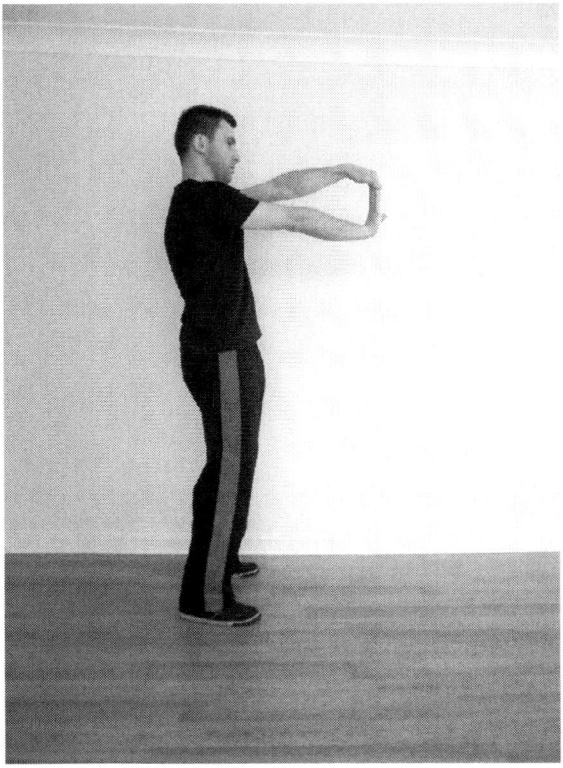

Torso & Back:

The torso and back areas are the most important part of our body for generating power in striking arts. The core muscles here, while perhaps not moving as much as their counterparts in the limbs are essential in keeping healthy and strong.

Trunk Side-Bend

Stand with both feet spread to shoulder width. Put both arms above your head. Grab the opposite elbow with each hand. Now carefully tip first toward the right without bending your knees. Hold for 15 seconds and then tip toward the left. Come back into center to complete your first rep.

For an alternate similar exercise, move your body in the same way but reach out to each side with the highest arm as you alternate from side to side.

Fore and Afts

To begin, arrange your body so that you are standing with the feet spread to shoulder width. Place your hands on the coordinating hips or to the sides of the head. Slowly tip forward and then back. Pay close attention to your body and each subtle motion. This stretch focuses on the abdominal and back regions.

Note: Do not tug the head forward and back. The hands are there for position purposes only, the body is doing the work.

Upper Back Flex

Begin either in a seated or standing position. Carefully flex your right arm before pushing it straight across your body. Grab your right tricep in the left hand. Now gently ease it a bit further into a nice stretch. Hold for a count of 15 before releasing.

Perform the stretch again on the left side, repeating the process.

Note: To make the stretch effective try to maintain a straight arm while gently pulling it across the body.

Forward Samurai Stretch

For this stretch you may need a soft surface to work on. Sit down on your knees, being sure to keep your feet touching, and toes aimed backward. Tip your body toward the floor, while simultaneously moving your hands along the floor as far out ahead as you can reach. Rest your head on the floor between your arms, relaxing each shoulder. Hold this stretch for a 15 count before carefully coming back up.

As always only push as far as you are comfortable. If you cannot reach your head to the ground just do what you can.

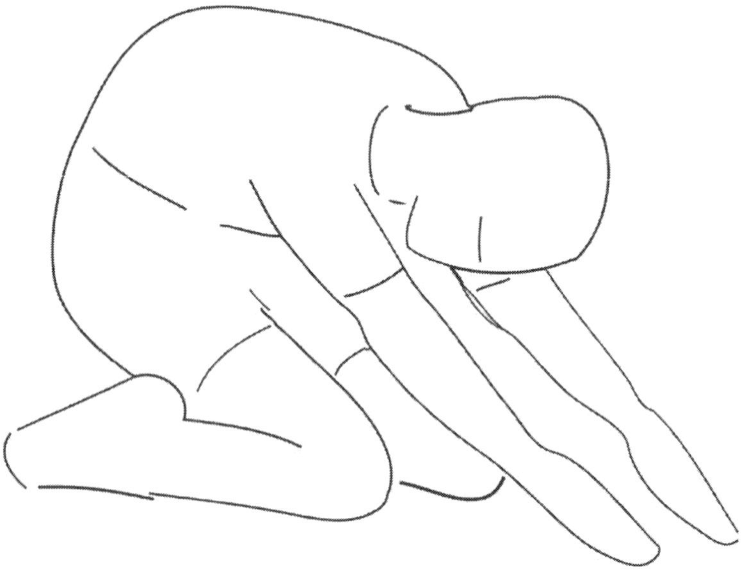

Back Press

To start, lie down and allow your body to relax. Now bend both knees, keeping the bottoms of your feet in contact with the floor. Gently push down toward the floor with the base of your back. Breathe in and out as you hold this position for a count of 15 and repeat five to ten times.

If you are familiar with Yoga, the form of this stretch is similar to Savasana.

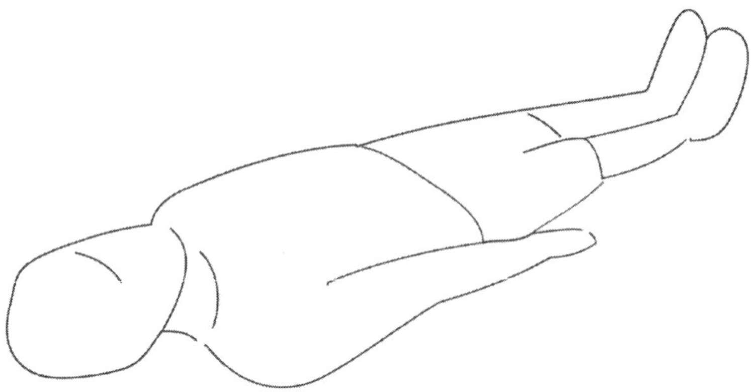

Trunk Twist

First sit with both hands placed just behind your head. Your elbows should be aimed out toward each side. Rotate from your core first towards the right to the point of resistance, hold for a moment then return to front before rotating toward the left and hold for about 15 seconds. Finish by coming back to center.

As before, the body drives the movement, not the hands. The hands are simply there for position purposes.

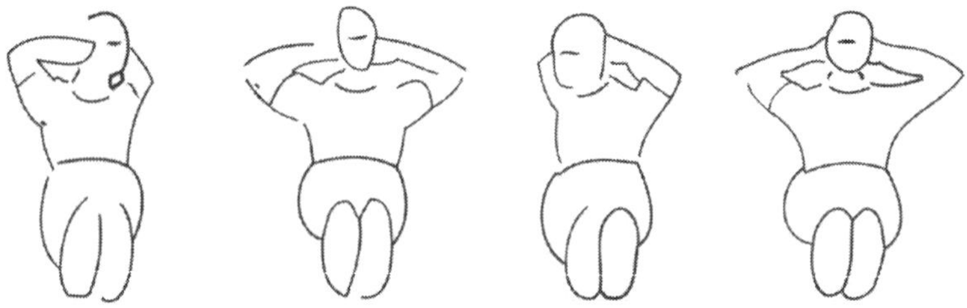

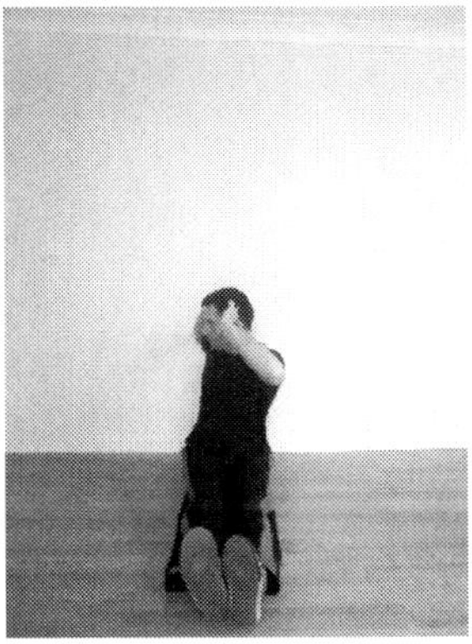

Cobra Stretch

Again borrowed from Yoga but a great all-round stretch. To get in the proper Cobra position, begin in a relaxed pose, lying on the floor, keeping both arms at your sides.

Shift so the palm of each hand rests flat against the floor, in line with your shoulders. Press against the floor to bring your chest and stomach up. Simultaneously arch your back. Gradually twist your neck first to the left, and then to the right. Come back to face forward before relaxing back to the floor.

Note: This exercise should be done slowly and carefully to avoid any potential risk to the back.

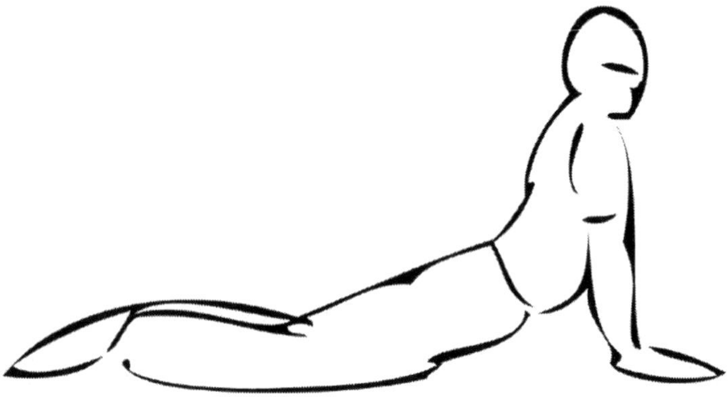

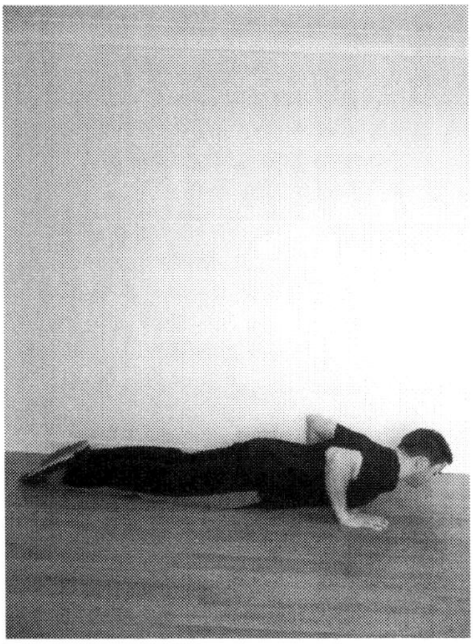

Side Stretch

Choose whether you would like to try this one in an upright or seated position. Get comfortable, and then reach both arms up above your head. Your arms should be as straight as possible without locking at the elbows. Intertwine the fingers of both hands with the palms facing up.

Reach your hands up as though you were reaching for the sky. Maintain a straight back while tipping slightly to the right beginning from your waist. Stay here for a count of 15. Return to start before repeating the stretch toward the opposite side.

Hip Adductor Extension

While this exercise may appear to work the legs (and it does slightly), the main purpose is to stretch the often tight hip adductor muscles that connect the thighs to the lower back and pelvis region.

Begin standing with both feet spaced about shoulder width apart. Flex the right leg while sinking the rest of your body toward the floor and gently pushing your left leg straight out to the side; utilize your arms to keep steady if needed. Try to maintain a straight back during this motion.

You can hold for 15 seconds on each leg or slowly alternate from side to side rocking the hips each way.

Leg-Straddle

Sit so that your knees are flexed and pointing away from the body. Remember to relax. It is ok if the outside portion of your legs cannot touch the floor in this position, though some people may find this easy.

Reach both arms out as though you were reaching for something in front of you. Then tilt forward. Stay here for a count of 15 before carefully coming back to start.

Repeat five to ten times in a gentle motion.

Spinal Twists

This is a stretch typically found in many Yoga practices but offers a great all round lower back stretch for any exercise.

Start on the floor, from the seated position, with legs straight ahead. Hold your head and torso straight and tall. Now put the right foot over to the left of your left knee. Move your left elbow to the right of the right knee. Place your right hand behind your body as far as possible comfortable reach. To initiate the stretch, press your right knee toward the left simultaneously twisting to the right at the shoulders. Keep this stretch for a 15 count before coming back into start.

Rest for a moment before repeating on the opposite side.

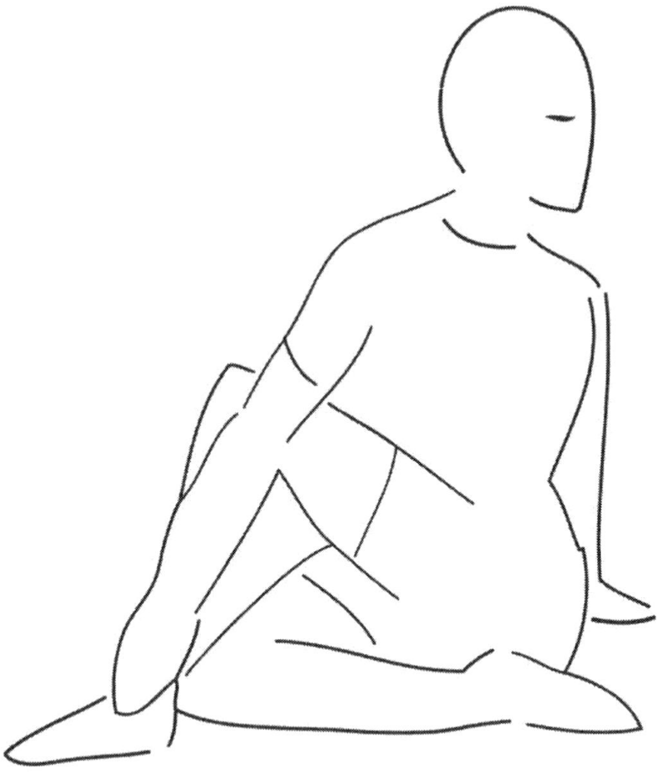

Chest

The chest can be a tricky area to isolate muscle groups in specifically. However those students whose training frequently includes push-ups or other upper body strength exercises should take time to gently stretch this area to improve muscle recovery.

High Left, High Right

First, make both hands into fists or open palms. Then move one upward above your head and the second near the coordinating hip. Bring your arms backward to initiate a stretch across the chest region. To make one full repetition try easing them to the right twice and then to the left an additional two times.

Push, Push, Throw

Lift both arms up in front of you so that they become parallel with the floor. Quickly tug both elbows towards your back two times. Complete a third tug while also turning your palms up to face the ceiling and stretching the arms out.

Alternatively point the fingers up at the point of extension, with palms facing outwards each time.

Gently return to start or repeat as required.

How to Stretch the Lower Body

These are the stretches that really benefit those in the kicking arts. TaeKwonDo, Karate and many styles of Shaolin Kung Fu often require mid-high level kicks and regular practice of these stretches can prevent injury and improve leg flexibility.

However it's not just Martial Artists that benefit from lower body work. Runners, Cyclists and anyone regularly utilizing their legs during intense exercise will get something from these.

Hamstrings & Quadriceps

Forward Lunge

Stand in a normal relaxed pose then take one giant step ahead with your right foot. Bend the right knee while keeping the left leg straight, but not over-locked. Place both hands on your hips, or on one knee, if you need to maintain control as you drop your hips forward and downward.

Stay with the stretch for a count of 15 before coming back into standing. Repeat, this time stepping forward with the other leg.

Reclined Knee Flex

Start by assuming a reclined position on the floor or an exercise mat. Grab your right knee and lift it towards your chest. Sustain the stretch for about a 15 second count before relaxing your leg back to start.

Repeat 3-4 times then complete the same on the other leg.

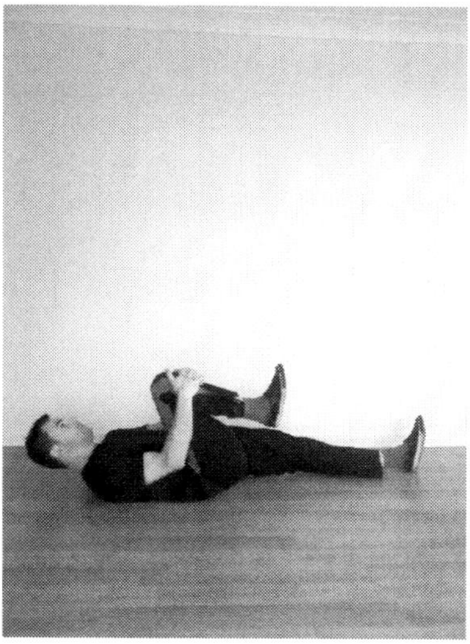

Dynamic Knee-Crunch

Begin standing so that your feet are spread by shoulder width. Gradually bring one of your knees up to your chest, or to the point of resistance. Then return the knee back to its initial position.

Repeat 5-10 times and on both sides.

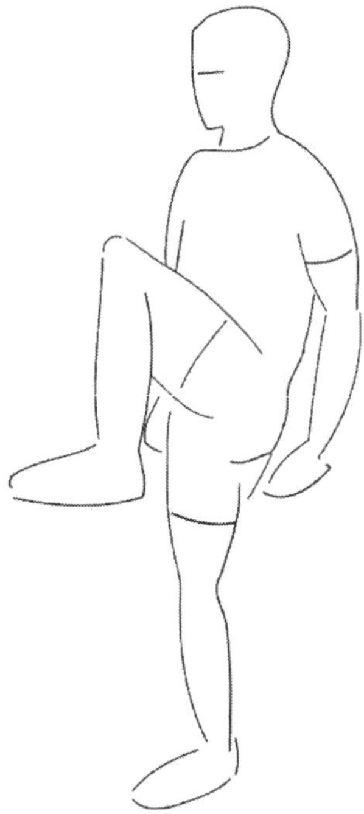

Basic Quadriceps Stretch

To do this stretch first choose a spot near a wall or chair in case you need additional stability.

Stand in a relaxed, but wide stance. Flex the left knee before raising the right foot behind you. Move your arms so that you are able to grab and hold the right foot with either one or both hands.

Tug gently to initiate a nice stretch. Hold for 15 seconds before carefully releasing the leg.

Note: You can add to this stretch by 'kicking' into the holding hand with about 20% power, then further stretching afterwards. Each engagement of the muscle helps the subsequent stretch.

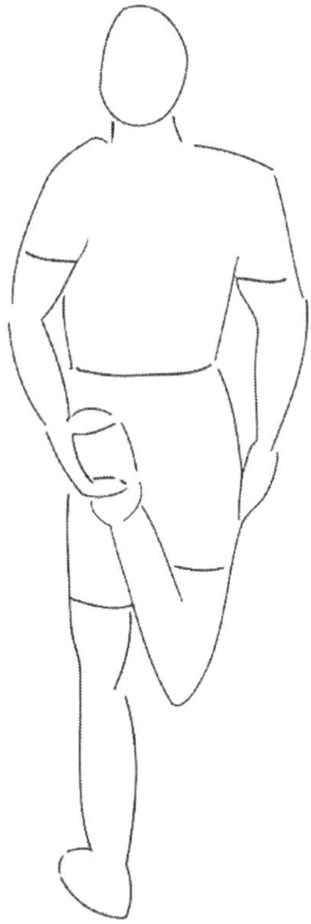

Reclined Quadriceps Stretch

This one is very similar to the basic quadriceps stretch as previously described. The only real difference is that it is done lying on one's stomach which makes balancing much easier!

In this version it is important to pay attention to hips and pelvis, being sure that they remain in contact with the floor and that it is the leg – not the back, which gets stretched.

Hurdles

Begin seated on the floor. Straighten both legs out. Move the right leg so that it rests behind you with the knee bent, and thigh touching the floor. (Ideally at a 90 degree angle) Gently tilt back to initiate a stretch in the quadriceps or lean into the open gap or outstretched leg to work the hips and hamstrings.

Hold for 15 seconds before relaxing upward then repeat on the other side as required.

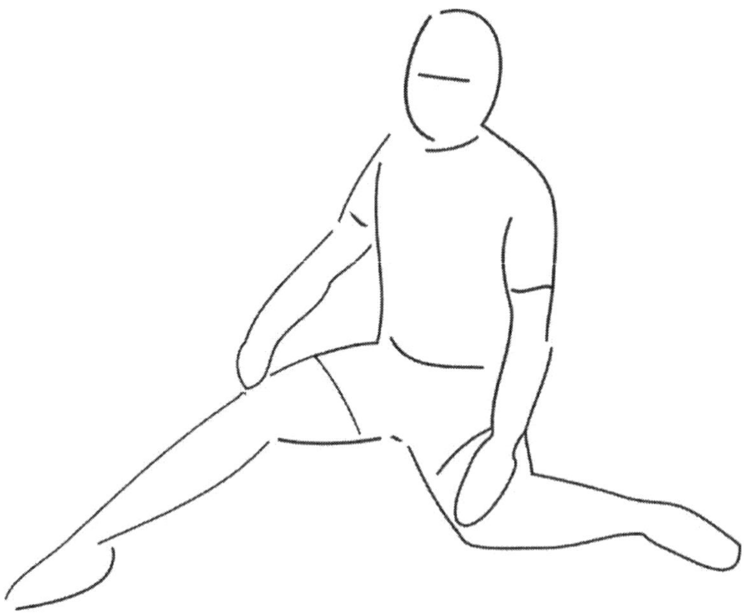

Hamstring Reach

Stand in your natural posture. Lean forward from the hips and bend your knees just a touch initially. Hold the stretch for a few moments then return to start. Once you are warmer attempt the same stretch with legs now straight.

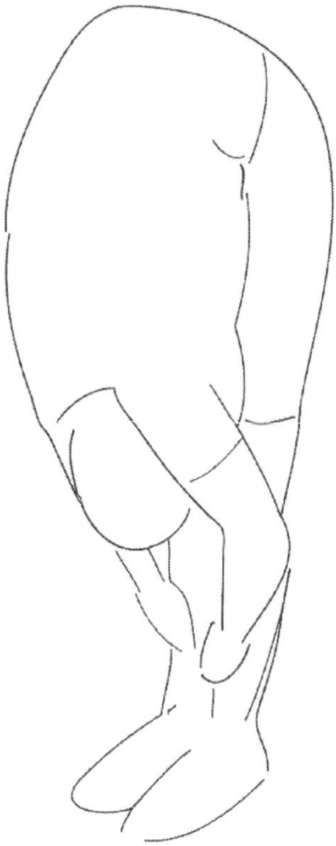

Hip Roll

The hip roll stretch is done lying down. Bring the right knee toward the left of your body. See if you can get it to touch the floor. From this pose, maintain floor contact with both shoulders as well.

Now count to 15 before releasing and repeating 5-10 times on both sides.

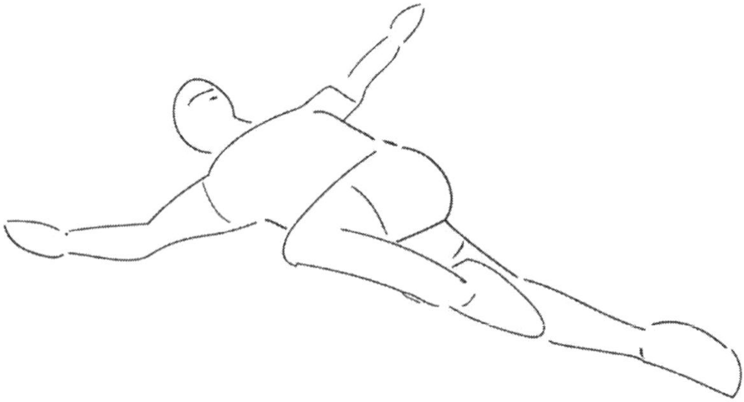

Double Hamstring Extension

Start out sitting tall so both legs are extended straight out. Stretch your hands forward, grasping your ankles or toes if you can. Now gradually lower your chest down to your knees. Keep the pose for a 15 count before relaxing back up to sitting.

Repeat 4-5 times or as required, relaxing between each motion.

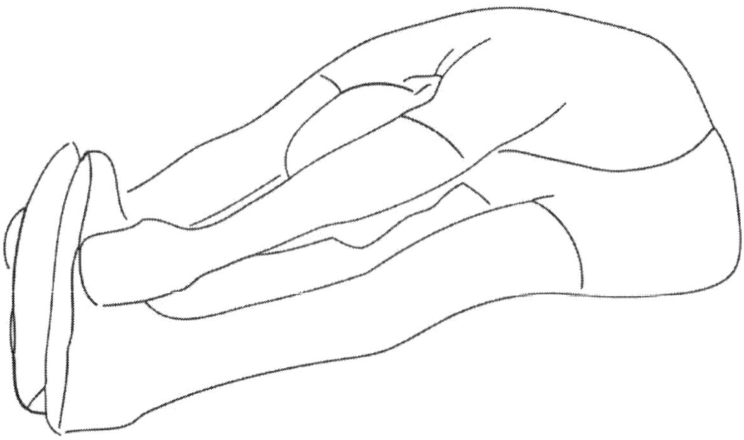

Reclined Hamstring Extension

As the name suggests, this one begins lying flat on the floor. Keep the left leg straight, but flex the right knee. Use both hands to grab the right knee to initiate a stretch in the hamstring. Carefully extend the knee, straightening your left leg. Momentarily maintain this stretch before coming back to start the next repetition on the opposite side.

Single Hamstring Extension

Sit down on the floor. Straighten the left leg, but bend the right. Tilt forward until you meet the point of resistance or your chest meets the left knee. Feel the stretch through a count of at least 10 seconds but ideally no more than 20. Gently come back up to start and repeat for both legs.

Butterfly

This easy stretch is performed sitting on the floor. Bring your feet together so that the soles meet. Hold your feet with both hands, and press the elbows against your knees. You should feel a stretch in the groin area. Stay in this pose for about a 10 second count before releasing and repeating.

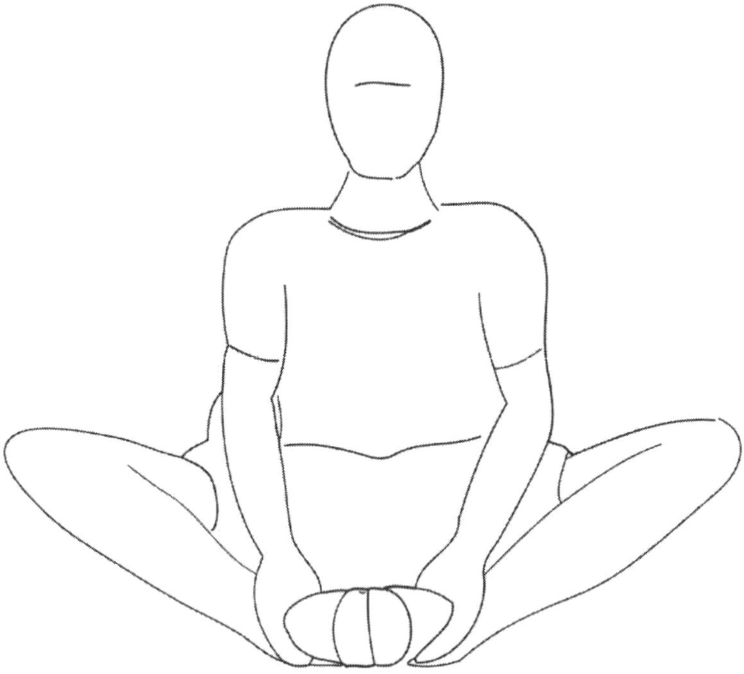

"V" Stretch

This stretch is one of the most popular within TaeKwonDo and kicking arts like Kickboxing.

Seat yourself on the ground. Stretch your legs into a V shape before spreading them to the point of resistance. Sit up tall then bend down until your chest grazes your left leg and hold this position. Rotate over to your right leg, hold again. Then return to a middle, position between both legs, before rising back up to the beginning pose.

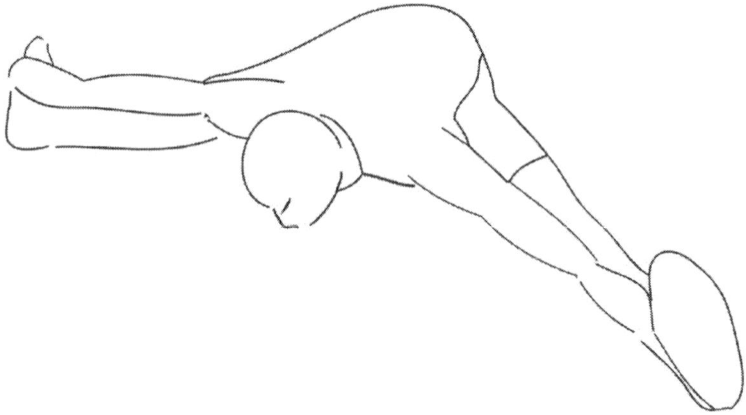

Iliotibial (IT) Band Stretch

Find a wall and separate yourself by a couple feet. Now place the right leg over the left. Move your right arm toward the wall and tilt. Reach out with your right hand until the palm makes contact and then let your bodyweight follow. Be sure that the right elbow and knee remain straight but not locked. Press both hips in as well. Hold the stretch for a count of 15 before releasing.

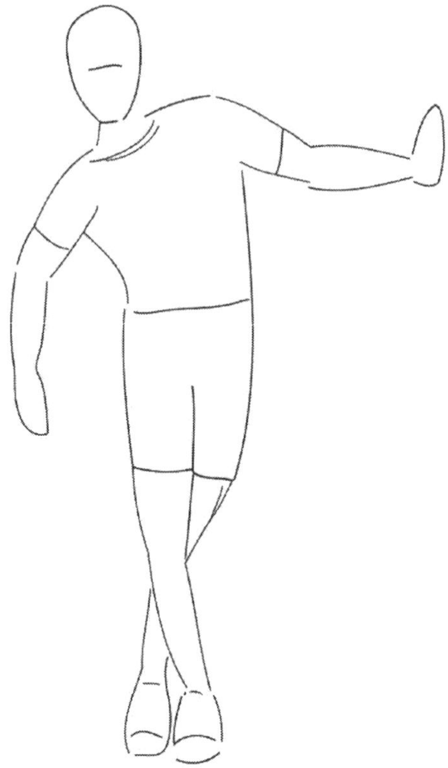

Cherry Picker

This fun stretch is done standing with feet spread to about double shoulder width. Reach down to the floor with both hands, as if you were reaching to harvest a nice ripe cherry. Stay here for five seconds. Now, move your hands just behind each coordinating leg. Enjoy this stretch for an additional five seconds.

Complete the series by pressing both hands toward the floor at the spot between your legs. Stay here for a final five seconds before rolling back up to start.

Calves & Ankles:

The lower leg is often overlooked in flexibility terms because of the smaller muscle groups but looseness in the Gastrocnemius and Soleus especially can help in kicking ability and reaction speed.

Calf Stretch

Stand with the front of your body towards, and about 3 feet away from a wall or the back of a chair. Arrange one leg just ahead of the other. Tilt your body toward the wall or chair while ensuring that your rear heel stays against the floor. Feel a stretch of your calf for a 15 second count. Repeat on the opposite side.

Samurai Stretch 2

Start out kneeling on a blanket or exercise mat. Ensure that your ankles and feet remain touching, with the toes aimed backward. Gradually, sit back further on your heels. Press both ankles deeper into the mat. Keep this stretch for a count of 15 seconds. Then relax onto your hands and knees to relieve the ankles and shins.

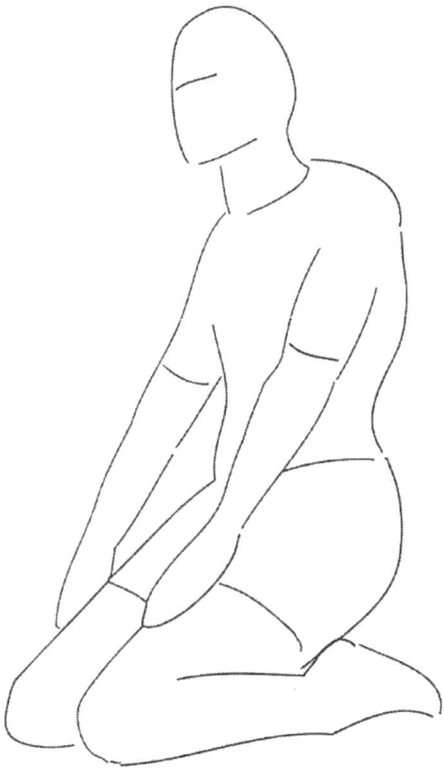

Bending Toe Raise

Stand with the left foot ahead of the right so that the heel of the left rests about twelve inches in front of the right toes. Bend the left foot back, then release.

Ensure that both legs stay straight, but not locked, and tilt your whole body until the chest touches the left leg, or you meet the point of resistance. Hold for 15 seconds before releasing.

Now try it on the other side.

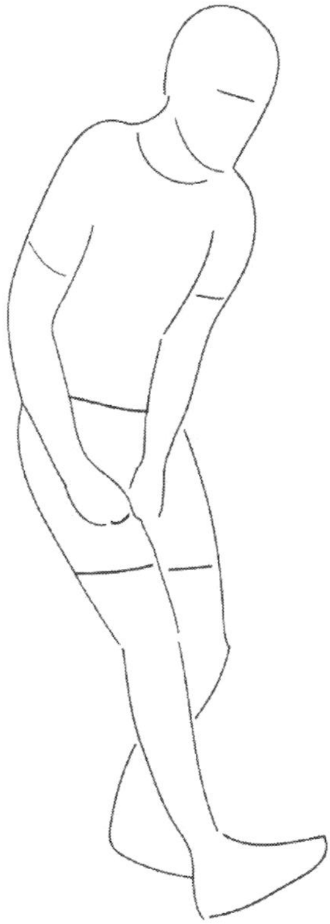

Compound Stretches

Compound stretches are great to work multiple muscle groups in one movement. Combining a few of these can help with a whole body warm-up.

Swordsman

Stand in a naturally wide stance. Take one giant step forward with the left leg. Bend the coordinating knee, keeping the right leg straight. Lift the right arm out in front of you. Now move the left leg back. Press your palms forward and back to initiate a nice trunk stretch. Now move back into start before repeating the stretch with the opposite footing.

Windmill

Lift both arms out toward their respective sides. Fold down so that the fingers of your right hand come in contact with the toes of your left foot. Hold this for approximately 15 seconds then come back up to center. Now fold down to the opposite side and repeat. Hold before coming back up to standing.

This exercise can be done slightly quicker from side to side as a more dynamic warm up.

Leg Swings

One of the staple warm ups of Martial Arts, legs swings are a great dynamic exercise for loosening the legs and stretching the hamstrings.

Start in either a guarding stance or with hands at your sides relaxed. Take one leg back straight, while the other is bent in front. Proceed to swing the rear leg up directly ahead of you, ensuring to keep the leg straight to enhance the stretch. Repeat for a 10 count on each leg.

Side Leg Swings

Side legs swings work in an almost identical way to front leg swings except that these help work a different set of muscles – ideal for styles using a lot of side-kicks (TaeKwonDo for example).

Start facing front with hands either up guarding or relaxed at your side. Then, keeping the foot pointing forwards and leg straight, swing the leg up to your side and repeat up to Ten times. (Turn the head to look at the foot if this helps).

This again is a dynamic exercise ideal for warming up the lower body and kicking muscles.

Extras

There are hundreds of potential stretches for every body part, and it would be unrealistic to list them all here. The following are a couple of additional exercises to attempt if you already find the others easy.

Rear Roll

While lying down on the floor lift your legs up into the air and over above your head. Push your torso back to the point of resistance. If you are able, touch the floor with your toes. Keep the stretch for 15 seconds before carefully allowing your legs to come back down.

Triangle

The starting position is similar to a push-up, the chest and legs should rest against the floor. Your palms should also rest against the floor, just below your shoulders. Push down and back so that the arms straighten and your backside lifts upward. Check to be sure your palms, shoulders, and body all line up. You can ask a friend to check your form. This is called a triangle because your body forms a "V", with the floor forming the third side. You should feel a stretch in your leg and back muscles.

Back Bow (Bridge)

The Back Bow is a fabulous stretch to enhance your martial arts training, although this challenge is best saved for those with advanced flexibility.

To begin, lay on the floor with both your arms and legs extended. Bend your knees to bring the bottom of each foot flat against the floor. Now move one hand to each side of your head, with the palms facing down. Make sure your fingers are aimed toward your feet. Press against the floor with both your hands and feet to lift your torso into the air. You will notice a nice stretch to your abs as your back begins to arc. Stay here for a count of 15 before gradually lowering back to the floor.

Feel the Burn...but not the snap!

Ask any modern Physiotherapist or Sports Massage practitioner and they will tell you that one of the most common misconceptions regarding physical manipulation is the ethos of:

"It has to hurt to help me"

Or

"No pain, no gain"

These old-school approaches to physical exercise were designed in their day to generate a tougher mental attitude to endurance and inspire athletes beyond their normal capacity. In this regard they were very successful and speaking to anyone of an older generation will show you the kind of fortitude required for training in the old days.

What they are unlikely to tell you are the injury rates and how many people were permanently damaged or forced to give up their aspirations of athletic greatness due to long term damage.

Martial Arts in particular have a silly history of physical torture for students, just as a means to demonstrate how tough they are. Sitting in Horse stance for 10 minutes as a Kung Fu student has a small benefit of strengthening the quadriceps weighed against the large pitfall of long term muscle damage.

This ethos of pain for the sake of pain in fitness is thankfully, slowly being replaced by intelligent approaches to training that, while still exhausting and often difficult, are not catalysts for injury and long-term damage as they would have been 30 years ago.

Today studies have shown through meticulous research that many 'old' training methods are outdated and offer little gain for the athlete.

Pushing yourself beyond the pain barrier is fine when it comes to cases of endurance but in stretching terms knowing your own limits is crucial to sustaining a healthy lifestyle and avoiding injury.

This isn't to say every exercise that has been around longer than 10 years has no value. Indeed Push-ups are still regarded by most to be one of the best full body exercises ever invented. But most modern studies show that once the body is indicating a pain response it is worthwhile listening to.

A marathon runner may get away with pushing past their limits. A Martial Artist trying to stretch for the splits should not!

How to Stretch the Full Body (Routines)

The following sequences are simple routines that work your entire body from top to toe. One focusing on the torso and arms, the other the legs and abdomen. Try them both for an overall quick and easy warm up.

As a starting point these movements are an excellent way to introduce your body to the exercise it will soon undertake and increase circulation to those areas soon to be engaged in hard work.

Practiced at an average pace, each sequence should take 3-5 minutes. With this in mind they also work well as a quick and uplifting warm-up for everyday use, either first thing in the morning as a way to wake up, or when you have a spare 5- 10 minutes during the day.

Upper Body

This Dynamic sequence focuses on loosening the muscles and joints from the head and neck downwards through the torso and arms. Perfect if you practice an upper-body heavy art like Wing Chun Kung Fu, Boxing or a Fitness regime involving weights.

Begin standing in a relaxed position. Feet roughly shoulder width apart.

1. **Start slowly by rotating your neck head, left, right, up and down and then slowly in a circle three to four times. (see Neck Stretches)**

2. **Next extend your arms and swing them in big circles forward 10 times and backwards 10 times.**

3. **Swing your arms across your chest so they cross over and back out to each side 10 times.**

4. **Push, Push Swing exercise (See Chest stretches section) 5 times**

5. **Keeping the arms bent and at shoulder height twist your torso to the left and right, looking over your shoulder on each count. (5 on each side)**

6. **Trunk side bends and Fore and Afts (See Torso and Back - 5 of each)**

7. **With hands on your hips slowly make a circle with the waist 5 times in each direction**

Lower Body

The lower body sequence runs through the main joints of the hip and knees; perfect for those involved in kick heavy styles like TaekwonDo or Kickboxing or for runners and people practicing leg-intensive sports.

Working down we start from the previous exercise, standing with hands on our hips in a relaxed position.

A great way to start on the lower body is to jog on the spot for 30 seconds.

1. Then, bring the knee up to the chest and make 5 circles clockwise, 5 circles counter-clockwise. Then repeat on the other leg.

2. Taking one leg straight back and complete 10 straight leg swings (See Leg Swings Exercise) to the front then repeat on the other leg.

3. Complete 10 leg swings to the side on both legs.

4. Next side bend to each side approximately 5 times; only this time we reach down with an extended hand – aiming to reach for the ankle.

5. Now, move into the Hip Adductor Extension position and gently rock from side to side, extending the outstretched leg fully each time

6. Hold one leg extended to the side and bend into the outstretched leg for a 10 count. Repeat on the other side.

7. After further gentle rocking from side to side extend both legs out to the as wide as you can. Hold this position for a moment.

8. With legs extended, reach down and place your palms on the floor (See Cherry Picker exercise) Hold for 10 seconds.

9. Keeping legs wide, ease yourself into a seated 'V' position.

10. In the V Position alternate reaching down to the left leg, right leg and center. To make it more dynamic do this to a ten-count with each position held for a shorter amount of time.

The 'Trick' to True Flexibility

Keeping Regular

There is a distinct and proven tactic to developing truly flexible joints and limbs.

If you are looking at Olympic Gymnasts or World Class Martial Artists as an example you will see they all have one common element of their training; regularity.

We're not talking about how much fiber they eat - rather how often they practice the techniques and stretches detailed in this guide.

For any fitness regime, stretching plan, Martial Arts training or weight loss scheme the single most important element is how often you stick to the plan. It might not sound like a 'trick' in the traditional sense but it's shocking how many people believe intensity is more important than regularity.

The fact is that doing an insane fat burning, body building super workout once every 2 weeks is good. Doing an average, modest level of exercise 5 times during that same period is better.

Constantly dreading your occasional workout will only lead to frustration and the eventual dropping of said sessions.

Intense, irregular stretching sessions or workouts every now and then are very taxing for the body but regular, lower intensity plans introduce the body to a new way of working and, in turn, allow it to change and adapt to a better more healthy lifestyle.

Once you reach the level of flexibility or fitness you want, the intensity suddenly becomes far less while the regularity easily increases.

The aim with all of this is to develop a pattern. A daily, or perhaps twice weekly routine, that becomes second nature; a part of your life. Once this is achieved you will one day notice that without even really thinking about it you can now do the splits, or run 10 miles or perform whatever goal you had in mind.

Basically, to be successful, get regular!

Thank You (and a Free Book!)

It's important to remember that slow and steady progress is the key to any improvements in flexibility. Some people are naturally gifted but the rest of us need to have patience in our approach. Take your time, work methodically and soon you will see great results!

Thanks for reading this guide. I work hard to create easy to follow guides for Martial Arts, Fitness and Self Defense.

I always appreciate your feedback so please give this book 5 stars if you found it useful! Good reviews mean the world to me and I try to respond to every one.

Finally, for a **COMPLETELY FREE** Training Guide check out my site at:

www.BlackBeltFit.com

Thanks again and good luck!

- Phil

Other Books by Phil Pierce

Check out some of the other Martial Arts, Fitness, and Well-Being titles from Phil Pierce:

Fitness Hacks: 50 Shortcuts to Effortlessly Cheat Your Way to a Better Body Today!

http://bit.ly/OHpkcr

Discover 50 Simple Shortcuts for more motivation, losing fat, building muscle, and a healthier, happier body today!

'Fitness Hacks' reveals the powerful secret tips and tricks YOU can easily use in your daily life to Lose Weight, Build Muscle, or get fit fast! This expert guide, with insights from top instructors, fitness coaches, and cutting-edge research skips the BS and hard work and exposes the efficiency shortcuts and psychological "hacks" you can use right now to improve your body today!

How to Meditate in Just 2 Minutes: Easy Meditation for Beginners and Experts Alike

http://bit.ly/1dYjnz6

Given, Meditation can be an incredibly powerful tool in improving both physical and mental health, focus, and relaxation, but most people think it takes a long time to see results. The truth is, it doesn't!

With this easy-to-use book, you can quickly learn how to achieve these incredible benefits in just 2 Minutes a day…

32286220R00070

Printed in Great Britain
by Amazon